LEARNING

for the
Christian
family

ABOUT SEX

Why Boys & Girls Are Different

For **Boys** ages **4-6** and **Parents**

CONCORDIA PUBLISHING HOUSE · SAINT LOUIS

Book 1 of the Learning about Sex Series

The titles in the series:

Book 1: Why Boys and Girls Are Different

Book 2: Where Do Babies Come From?

Book 3: How You Are Changing

Book 4: Sex and the New You

Book 5: Love, Sex, and God

Book 6: How to Talk Confidently with Your Child about Sex

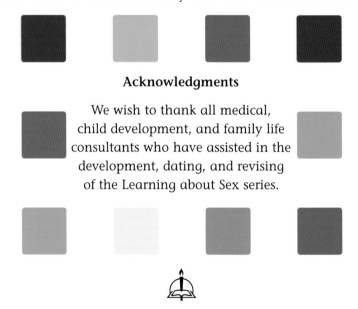

Acknowledgments

We wish to thank all medical, child development, and family life consultants who have assisted in the development, dating, and revising of the Learning about Sex series.

Copyright © 1982, 1988, 1995, 1998, 2008 Concordia Publishing House
3558 S. Jefferson Ave., St. Louis, MO 63118-3968
1-800-325-3040 • www.cph.org

From text originally written by Carol Greene

Illustrations by Michelle Dorenkamp

Unless otherwise indicated, all Scripture quotations are taken from The Holy Bible, English Standard Version®. Copyright © 2001 by Crossway Bibles, a publishing ministry of Good News Publishers, Wheaton, Illinois. Used by permission. All rights reserved.

This publication may be available in braille, in large print, or on cassette tape for the visually impaired. Please allow 8 to 12 weeks for delivery. Write to Lutheran Blind Mission, 7550 Watson Road, St. Louis, MO 63119-4409; call 1-888-215-2455; or visit the Web site: www.blindmission.org.

Manufactured in Heshan, China/047365/406705

2 3 4 5 6 7 8 9 1 0   1 7 1 6 1 5 1 4 1 3 1 2 1 1

Editor's Foreword

This book is one of a series of six designed to help parents communicate biblical values to their children in the area of sexuality. *Why Boys and Girls Are Different* is the first book in the series. It is written especially for boys ages four to six and, of course, for the parents, teachers, and other concerned grown-ups who will read the book to the child. (See the "Note to Grown-ups" at the end of the book for suggestions on using the book and ways to communicate Christian values in sex education in the home.)

Like its predecessor, the new Learning about Sex series provides information about the social-psychological and physiological aspects of human sexuality. But more importantly, it does so from a distinctively Christian point of view in the context of our relationship to the God who created us and redeemed us in Jesus Christ. The series presents sex as another good gift from God, which is to be used responsibly.

Each book in the series is graded in vocabulary and in the amount of information it provides. It answers the questions that persons at each age level typically ask.

Because children vary widely in their growth rates and interest levels, parents and other concerned adults will want to preview each book in the series, directing the child to the next graded book when he is ready for it.

In addition to reading each book, you can use them as starting points for casual conversation and when answering other questions a child might have.

This book can also be used as a mini-unit or as part of another course of study in a Christian preschool setting. Whenever the book is used in a class setting, it is important to let the parents know beforehand, since they have the prime responsibility for the sex education of their children. If used in a classroom setting, the books are designed for separate single-gender groups, the setting most conducive to open conversations about questions and concerns.

While parents will appreciate the help of the school, they will want to know what is being taught. As the Christian home and the Christian school work together, Christian values in sex education can be more effectively strengthened.

The Editors

I am a he.

God made me!

She's a she.

God made her too!

God made you too. He did a good job, didn't He?

Each of us is special. Each of us is loved by God.

You are you. And I am me.

I like to jump.

I like the color red.

I like vanilla ice cream cones.

In some ways, we are the same. In some ways, we're not.

God made us that way. I like God's plans.

And I like you.

You are you. And she is she.

She likes to hop.

She likes the color yellow.

She likes chocolate ice cream cones.

In some ways, we are the same. In some ways, we're not.

God made us that way. I like God's plans.

And I like you. I like her too.

God gave us eyes to see with

and ears to hear with

and noses to smell with

and mouths to talk and taste with.

God gave us hands and feet and fingers and toes.
He gave us laughter and minds to think with.

God made each one of us special but not the same.

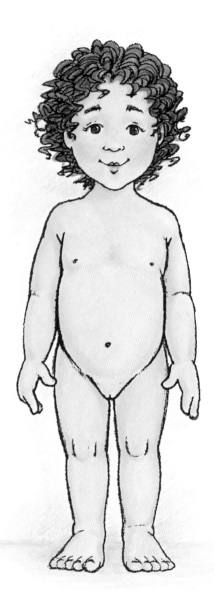

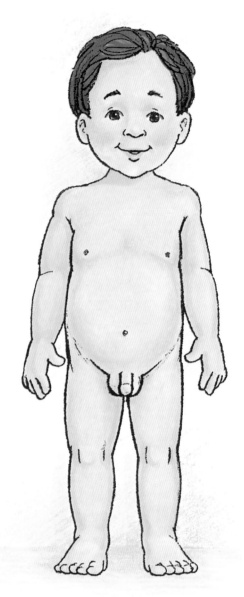

God gave girls a vagina.

It is on the inside.

That is the best place for it.

God gave boys a penis.

It is on the outside.

That is the best place for it.

God gave us wonderful bodies. All of God's gifts are good.

You know, God made a lot of shes,

and shes can do a lot of things.

His mother is a she.

So is his grandma, sister, and cousin . . .

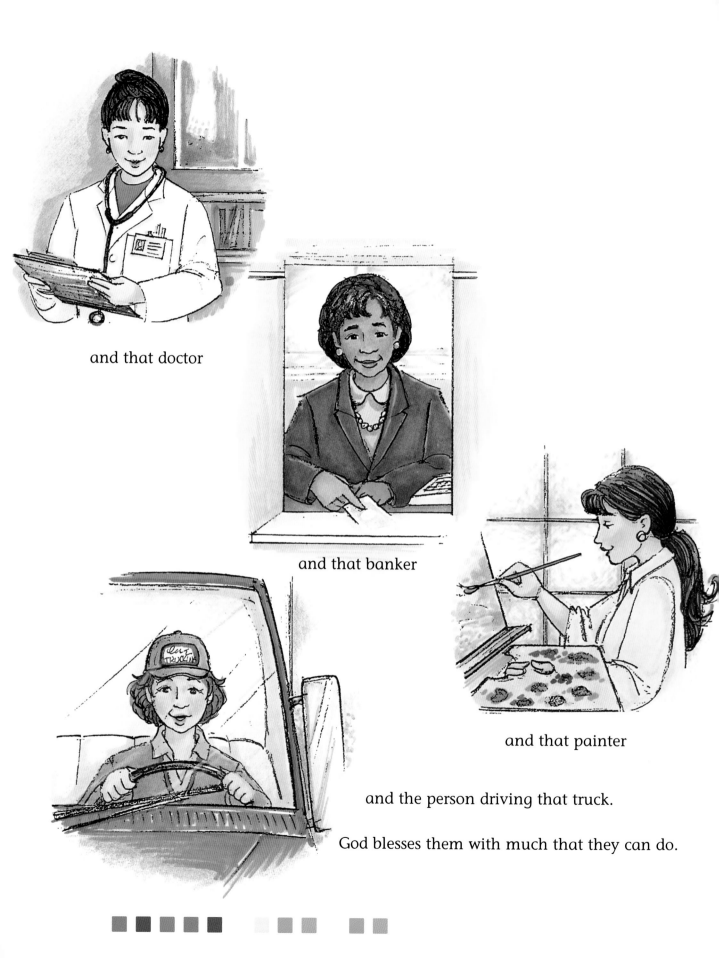

and that doctor

and that banker

and that painter

and the person driving that truck.

God blesses them with much that they can do.

God made a lot of hes too,

and hes can do a lot of things.

Her father is a he.

So is her grandpa and her uncle . . .

and that firefighter

and that cook

and that teacher

and the person flying that plane.

God blesses them with much that they can do.

How did God make us?

I don't know. Let's ask.

God made you in a special way.

You see, sometimes a grown-up he and a grown-up she love each other very much. They want to be together all the time. So with God's blessing, they get married. Then, they decide they want a little baby to share their love.

The baby grows inside its mother for nine months. It is safe and warm. Sometimes, when it wiggles and kicks, you can feel it from the outside.

God is blessing
this growing family.

I think that's great!

Me too.

After nine months, the baby is born.

It comes out through the mother's vagina.

The whole family is very glad to see the new baby.

That is how God made YOU.

That is how He makes all people.

God blesses us in an important way.

He puts people in families.

That's so they can take care of each other

and love each other.

Some families are small.

Some families are big.

There are many different kinds of families.

I thank God for my family.

Let's thank God for your family too!

Families do things together.

He likes to play with his sisters.

He likes to go fishing with his grandpa.

He likes to go bike riding with his dad.

He's glad God put him into a family.

God blesses us with families.

She likes to sing songs with her mother.

She likes to play ball with her brother.

She likes to listen to her grandma's stories.

What do YOU like to do with YOUR family?

God puts us into a church family too.
People in church families share God's love.
They hear God's Word and sing His praises.

Some church families are small.

Some church families are big.

There are many different people in a church family.

But in some ways, we are the same.

We all are sinners. We all need Jesus to forgive us.

I'm glad God put me into a church family.

I like to learn that Jesus is my Savior.

I like to sing songs about Jesus who loves me.

I like to see my friends at church.

I like to pray to Jesus. He hears and helps me.

I like to know that God is always near.

What do YOU like about YOUR church family?

I am a he.

God made me!

She's a she.

God made her too!

God loves each one specially.

He knows your name. He knows mine too.

God is so good to us.

Thank God for all the blessings He gives
to every boy and to every girl!
He loves us all. He loves YOU too!

The End

"I praise [God], for I am fearfully and wonderfully made. Wonderful are Your works!" Psalm 139:14

A Note to Grown-ups

We're all aware of the stereotypical adult responses to a toddler's first question about sex. There's embarrassment: "Er, uh, go ask your mother." There's evasion: "Mommy thinks she hears the telephone." And there's the flight of fancy: "Once there was a big white bird . . ."

Of course, you aren't a stereotype. But you may be one of the many adults who prefer to approach their children's questions with the aid of other resources. This book is designed to provide that aid and to do so in a Christian context.

But no one book can anticipate the needs of all preschoolers. Ultimately, adults must rely on their own sensitivity and common sense. A few pointers, however, may help.

First and foremost, remember that sexuality is far more than the reproductive organs with which each of us is born. It is a tremendous gift from God and colors almost everything we are and do. The sense of joy and wonder you feel in your own sexuality and that of your child is one of the most important things you can teach him.

Ideally, children would grow up in a home with two parents who openly show their love and respect for one another and for their children, where each person in the family is valued for who she or he is. But this isn't an ideal world, and many single parents must cope without the aid of a spouse. If that is your situation, try to spend time with a special friend or relative of the other sex, and let your child be part of the interaction. Or try to spend time with a couple in your extended family or church. Models are important for young children.

Now, back to that first question. Even if you are a bit nervous, let your child know that you're glad he came to you with questions. Curiosity is good; it helps us learn. Bear in mind that a child doesn't carry all the societal baggage attached to sex that adults do. Today, Sam wants to know more about his penis. Tomorrow, he may show equal curiosity about his teeth.

Listen carefully to the question, and be sure you understand it. (Remember the old joke? Bobby asks, "Mom, where did I come from?" Mom gives a carefully preplanned lecture on reproduction. Bobby looks bored. It turns out his best friend came from Memphis, and Bobby just wants to know where he came from.)

Once you understand the question, try to answer it in a precise, matter-of-fact way. If Josh wants to know why Mrs. Blackwell's tummy is so fat, explain that Mrs. Blackwell is going to have a baby. "But it isn't in her tummy. It's in a special place called the uterus, which God made for babies before they are born."

If Josh follows this with another question, answer it with equal honesty, and continue to do so until his curiosity is satisfied. In general, it's best to answer no more than the child asks. But don't berate yourself later if you think you've said too much. Most small children will absorb only as much information as they can handle.

Don't be surprised, by the way, if Josh repeats the same series of questions tomorrow or three weeks from now. For a number of psychological reasons, small children thrive on repetition. But do be sure that you're consistent in the answers you give.

Also, be sure to use correct terminology with Josh during such discussions. This will let him know that you're taking him quite seriously. It may also prevent embarrassment later.

An area of confusion for some children involves their genitals and their organs of elimination. "They're all in the same place," reasons Sam. "And Mommy says to wash my hands after I go to the bathroom. So, they must all be dirty."

If your child thinks like Sam, explain that we wash our hands after going to the bathroom to get rid of any germs that are in a bowel movement. But that doesn't mean that any part of our body is dirty in a bad way. All the parts do just the job that God made them to do.

Unfortunately, you should also warn your child about the possibilities of abuse. You might want to work this into a discussion of appropriate behavior.

"Your body belongs to you, including those private parts that your swimming suit covers. You don't show those parts or touch them in public. And other people should not touch your private parts either. No one has a right to do that unless it's a nurse or a doctor helping you to be well or someone who cares for you helping you to be clean. If anyone does touch your private parts, be sure to tell me. I want to keep you safe."

Our world is bombarded with sexual references and exploitation. Not even a preschooler can escape that completely. But your child's trust still remains in you. You are the real authority to him or her in almost every matter, including sexuality. Your joy and wonder, respect and love will awaken similar responses in your child. Together you can marvel that "male and female He created them. . . . God saw everything that He had made . . . and it was very good" (Genesis 1:27, 31). And you can rejoice that through Jesus' saving grace, we can "see what kind of love the Father has given to us, that we should be called children of God" (1 John 3:1).